Contents

Gnome Home

Yarn 4

Bernat® *Sheep(ish)* by Vickie Howell, 3oz/85g balls, each approx 167yd/153m (acrylic/wool)
- 1 (1, 1, 2, 2) balls in Chartreuse(ish) #20 (A)
  - 1 ball Olive(ish) #0019 (B)
  - 1 ball Turquoise(ish) #17 (C)
  - 1 ball Pink(ish) #008 (D)
  - 1 ball Hot Pink(ish) #007 (E)
- Small amount of worsted weight black yarn

Needles

- One size 8 (5mm) circular needle, 16"/40.5cm long *or size to obtain gauge*
- One set (4) size 8 (5mm) double-pointed needles (dpns)
- One set (4) size 7 (4.5mm) double-pointed needles (dpns)
- One pair size 5 (3.75mm) needles
- One set (4) size 3 (3.25mm) double-pointed needles (dpns)

Notions

- Stitch markers
- Yellow embroidery thread
- Tapestry needle

SIZES
Newborn (6–12 mos, 1–2 yrs, 3–5 yrs, 6–10 yrs)

FINISHED MEASUREMENTS
Circumference 12 (15½, 17¼, 18¼, 19)"/30.5 (39.5, 44, 46.5, 48.5)cm

GAUGE
20 sts and 27 rnds = 4"/10cm in St st with largest needles.
Take time to check your gauge.

NOTES
1 Choose hat size with circumference 1½–2"/4–5cm smaller than actual head circumference.
2 Change to double-pointed needles when circumference gets too small for circulars.
3 House fixtures and flowers are worked separately and sewn in place.

STITCH GLOSSARY
Garter st Knit 1 rnd, purl 1 rnd.
I-cord With dpns, cast on designated number of sts or continue working with rem sts. *Knit one row. Without turning the work, slip the sts back to the beginning of the row. Pull the yarn tightly from the end of the row. Rep from the * as desired. Bind off.

HAT
With A and circular needle, cast on 56 (72, 80, 84, 88) sts. Join, being careful not to twist sts, and pm for beg of rnd.
Work 4 rnds in garter st.
Work in St st (k every rnd) until hat measures 2 (2, 2½, 2½, 2¾)"/5 (5, 6.5, 6.5, 7)cm from cast-on edge.

Shape crown
Rnd 1 [K12 (16, 18, 19, 20), k2tog, pm] 4 times—52 (68, 76, 80, 84) sts.
Rnd 2 Knit.
Rnd 3 [K to 2 sts before marker, k2tog] 4 times—4 sts dec.
Rep rnds 2–3 until 20 sts rem.
Change to smaller needles and rep rnds 2–3 until 8 sts rem.
Next rnd [K2tog] 4 times—4 sts.
Work 6 (6, 6, 10, 10) rows I-cord, bind off.

Door
With B and straight needles, cast on 6 sts. Work 10 rows in St st, bind off. With yellow embroidery thread, embroider a French knot on one side for the doorknob.

Windows (make 3)
With C and straight needles, cast on 4 sts. Work 4 rows in St st, bind off.

Small flowers (make 2 of each in C, D, and E)
With size 7 (4.5mm) dpns, cast on 4 sts, bind off 3 sts. [Slide last st over to left needle. Use knitted cast-on to cast on 3 sts. Bind off 3 sts] 4 times. Fasten off, use tail to gather petals together in center.

Large flowers (using colors C, D, and E, make 1 of each color)
With medium size dpns, cast on 6 sts, bind off 5 sts. *Slide last st over to left needle. Use knitted cast-on to cast on 6 sts, bind off 5 sts. Rep from * 3 times. Fasten off, use tail to gather petals together in center.

STEMS
Small (make 2)
With B and size 3 (3.25mm) dpns, cast on 3 sts, work 16 rows I-cord, bind off.

Long (make 2)
With B and size 3 (3.25mm) dpns, cast on 3 sts, work 22 rows I-cord, bind off.

FINISHING
Sew door to front of hat. Sew windows to front of hat, use photo as guide. With embroidery thread, line the windows and separate windows into 4 panes, as pictured. Curl stems into desired shape and sew onto hat around front and sides. Sew large flowers, plus one small flower, to top of stems. Sew small flowers around rim of hat and near door, as pictured. Using (3) 16"/40.5 cm strands for each cord, make 2 twisted cords with A. Make 2 tassels with A. Sew tassels to bottom of twisted cord. Sew twisted cord to sides of hat. ■

Feeling Sheepish

Yarn 6

Red Heart® *Light & Lofty*®, 6oz/170g skeins, each approx 140yd/128m (acrylic)
- 1 (1, 1, 1, 2) skeins in Puff #9316 (A)
- 1 skein in Café au Lait #9344 (B)

Red Heart® *Soft*, 5oz /141g balls, each approx 256yd/234m (acrylic)
- 1 skein in Pink #6768 (C)

Needles

- One size 15 (10mm) circular needle, 24"/61cm long *or size to obtain gauge*
- One pair size 11 (8mm) needles
- One pair size 15 (10mm) needles

Notions

- Stitch marker
- 2 Wood flower buttons 1⅛"/3cm in diameter
- Tapestry needle
- Stuffing

SIZES

Newborn (6–12 mos, 1–2 yrs, 3–5 yrs, 6–10 yrs)

FINISHED MEASUREMENTS

Circumference 11 (14, 16, 17, 18)"/28 (35.5, 40.5, 43, 45)cm

GAUGE

8 sts and 12 rows = 4"/10cm in Seed st with larger needles.
Take time to check your gauge.

NOTES

1 Choose hat size with circumference 2½–3"/6.5–7.5cm smaller than actual head circumference.
2 The cowl is worked in the rnd to length then hood is worked in rows.
3 The ears and tail are made separately and sewn in place.

STITCH GLOSSARY

Seed st (over an even number of sts)
Rnd/row 1 [K1, p1] to end.
Rnd/row 2 Purl the knits and knit the purls.
Rep rnd/row 2 for pat.

COWL

With B and circular needle, cast on 30 (34, 36, 40, 44) sts. Join, being careful not to twist sts, and pm for beg of rnd. Work 6 rnds in Seed st. Change to A and work in Seed st until cowl measures 7 (7, 7¼, 7½, 8)"/18 (18, 18.5, 19, 20.5)cm from cast-on edge.

Shape hood

Note Begin working in rows maintaining seed st pat.
Row 1 (RS) K1, ssk, work in seed st to last 3 sts, k2tog, k1—2 sts dec.
Row 2 (WS) Work even in seed st.
Rep last 2 rows 3 (2, 1, 2, 3) times—22 (28, 32, 34, 36) sts.
Work even in Seed st until hood measures 8 (9, 10, 11, 11)"/20.5 (23, 25.5, 28, 28)cm from 1st dec row. Graft hood together.

SHEEP EARS (MAKE 2)

Outer ear

With A and larger needles, cast on 7 sts.
Row 1 (RS) Kfb, knit to last st, kfb—9 sts.
Row 2 (WS) Purl.
Rows 3–8 Work even in St st.
Row 9 Ssk, knit to last 2 sts, k2tog—2 sts dec.
Row 10 Purl.
Rows 11–14 Rep rows 9–10—3 sts. Bind off.

Inner ear

With 2 strands of C held together and smaller needles, cast on 5 sts.
Row 1 (RS) Kfb, knit to last st, kfb—2 sts inc
Row 2 (WS) Purl.
Rows 3–4 Rep rows 1–2—9 sts.
Rows 5–8 Work even in St st.
Row 9 Ssk, knit to last 2 sts, k2tog—2 sts dec.
Row 10 Purl.
Rows 11–14 Rep rows 9–10—3 sts. Bind off.
With RS tog, backstitch inner ear to outer ear, leaving bottom edge open. Turn ear RS out and stuff lightly. Sew bottom edge together, cinching it to make a curved shape. With B and tapestry needle, whipstitch loosely around entire edge of ear, between the inner and outer line. Sew ears to side of hood, allowing to droop a bit.

Tail

With 2 strands of C held together and smaller needles, cast on 16 sts.
Rows 1–6, 8 and 10 Work even in Seed st

Rows 7 and 9 Ssk, work 12 sts, k2tog—2 sts dec. Cut yarn leaving a long tail, weave through rem sts, pull closed and secure end. Seam edges of tail tog, leaving a small opening. Stuff tail lightly, keeping it in a flat shape. Finish seaming tail and sew in place at back of cowl.

Edging

With WS facing and circular needle, and at a rate of 2 sts for every 3 rows, pick up and knit an even number of stitches around hood opening. Join and pm for beg of rnd. Work 6 rnds in Seed st, bind off, let edging curl. ■

Piglet Cap

SIZES
Newborn (6–12 mos, 1–2 yrs, 3–5 yrs, 6–10 yrs)

FINISHED MEASUREMENTS
Circumference 12 (16, 17¼, 18, 18¾)"/30.5 (40.5, 44, 45.5, 47.5)cm

GAUGE
12 sts and 18½ rnds = 4"/10cm in St st with larger needles.
Take time to check your gauge.

NOTES
1 Choose size with circumference 1½–3"/4–7.5cm smaller than actual head circumference.
2 Change to double-pointed needles when circumference gets too small for circulars.
3 Ears, tail, and nose are worked separately and sewn in place.

STITCH GLOSSARY
K1, p1 rib (over an even number of sts)
Rnd 1 [K1, p1] around.
Rnd 2 Knit the knits and purl the purls.
Rep rnd 2 for pattern.

I-cord With dpns, cast on designated number of sts or continue working with rem sts. *Knit one row. Without turning the work, slip the sts back to the beginning of the row. Pull the yarn tightly from the end of the row. Rep from the * as desired. Bind off.

HAT
With larger needles, cast on 36 (48, 52, 54, 56) sts. Join, being careful not to twist sts, and pm for beg of rnd.
Rnds 1–4 Work in k1, p1 ribbing.
Change to St st, work even until hat measures 4¼ (5¼, 4¼, 5½, 7)"/11 (13.5, 11, 14, 18)cm from cast-on edge.

Shape crown
Rnd 1 [K4 (6, 11, 7, 6) sts, k2tog] 6 (6, 4, 6, 7) times—30 (42, 48, 48, 49) sts.
Rnd 2 [K3 (5, 10, 6, 5) sts, k2tog] 6 (6, 4, 6, 7) times—24 (36, 44, 42, 42) sts.
Rnd 3 [K2 (4, 9, 5, 4) sts, k2tog] 6 (6, 4, 6, 7) times—18 (30, 40, 36, 35) sts.
Rnd 4 [K1 (3, 8, 4, 3) sts, k2tog] 6 (6, 4, 6, 7) times—12 (24, 36, 30, 28) sts.
Rnd 5 [K0 (2, 7, 3, 2) sts, k2tog] 6 (6, 4, 6, 7) times—6 (18, 32, 24, 21) sts.

Sizes 6–12 mos (1–2 yrs, 3–5 yrs, 6–10 yrs) ONLY
Rnd 6 [K1 (6, 2, 1) sts, k2tog] 6 (4, 6, 7) times—12 (28, 18, 14) sts.
Rnd 7 [K0 (5, 1, 0) sts, k2tog] 6 (4, 6, 7) times—6 (24, 12, 7) sts.

Sizes 1–2 yrs (3–5 yrs) ONLY
Rnd 8 [K4 (0) sts, k2tog] 4 (6) times—20 (6) sts.

Size 1–2 yrs ONLY
Rnd 9 [K3, k2tog] 4 times—16 sts.
Rnd 10 [K2, k2tog] 4 times—12 sts.
Rnd 11 [K1, k2tog] 4 times—8 sts.
Rnd 12 K2tog 4 times—4 sts.

All sizes
Cut yarn leaving a long tail, weave through rem sts, pull closed and secure end.

Piglet ears (make 2)
With larger needles, cast on 5 sts.
Row 1 (RS) K2, p1, k2.
All WS rows K1, purl to last st, k1.
Row 3 K1, kfb, k1, p1, k1, kfb, k1—7 sts.

Row 5 K1, kfb, k2, p1, k2, kfb, k1—9 sts.
Rows 7 and 9 K5, p1, k5.
Row 11 K1, ssk, k2, p1, k2, k2tog, k1—7 sts.
Row 13 K1, ssk, p1, k2tog, k1—5 sts.
Row 15 Ssk, p1, k2tog—3 sts.
Row 17 S2KP—1 st. Fasten off.

Piglet nose
With larger needles, cast on 6 sts.
Row 1 (RS) [K1, kfb] 3 times—9 sts.
All WS Rows Purl.
Row 3 [K1, kfb, kfb] 3 times—15 sts.
Row 5 [K1, kfb] 7 times, k1—22 sts.
Row 7 Knit.
Row 9 [K1, k2tog] 7 times, k1—15 sts.
Row 11 [K1, k2tog, k2tog] 3 times—9 sts.
Row 13 [K1, k2tog] 3 times—6 sts.
Cut yarn leaving a long tail, weave through rem sts, pull closed and secure end.

Piglet tail
With smaller dpns, cast on 2 sts. Work 6½"/16.5cm I-cord. Fasten off.

FINISHING
Sew ears in place at top of hat, pinching base just a little to cup the ears into shape. Sew snout along seam, leaving a small opening. Stuff lightly into a slightly flat, round shape, then finish seam. Use embroidery thread to sew buttons into place on snout, going all the way through the back and pulling tight to draw in the nostrils. Sew snout to hat. With embroidery thread, embroider eyes as pictured. Curl tail with fingers, then sew into place at back of hat above ribbing. ■

Magical Moose Cap

Yarn 🌀5

Red Heart® Boutique™ Swirl™, 3oz/85g balls, each approx 106yd/97m (polyester/acrylic/wool/alpaca)
- 1 (1, 1, 1, 2) balls in Linen #9301 (A)
- 1 ball in Cobblestone #9311 (B)

Needles

- One size 11 (8mm) circular needle, 16"/40.5cm long *or size needed to obtain gauge*
- One set (4) size 11 (8mm) double-pointed needles (dpns)

Notions

- Stitch markers
- Tapestry needle
- 2 brown shank buttons ½"/1.5cm in diameter
- Sewing needle and thread
- Black embroidery thread
- 2 pipe cleaners
- Stuffing
- Tweezers

SIZES

Newborn (6–12 mos, 1–2 yrs, 3–5 yrs, 6–10 yrs)

FINISHED MEASUREMENTS

Circumference 12½ (15¼, 16¾, 18, 18¾)"/32 (38.5, 42.5, 45.5, 47.5)cm

GAUGE

11½ sts and 20 rnds = 4"/10cm in Seed st with size 11 (8mm) needles.
Take time to check your gauge.

NOTES

1 Choose the size with circumference 1–2¾"/2.5–7cm smaller than actual head circumference.
2 Hat is worked in seed stitch, maintain the stitch pattern as closely as possible when increasing or decreasing.
3 The muzzle is shaped by working back and forth in rows.
4 Twist yarns around each other when changing colors to prevent holes in the work.
5 Change to dpns when circumference gets too small for circulars when shaping crown.
6 The ears and antlers are worked separately and sewn in place.
7 Pipe cleaners are used in the antlers for stability.

STITCH GLOSSARY

Seed stitch (over an even number of sts)
Rnd 1 [K1, p1] around.
Rnd 2 Knit the purls and purl the knits
Rep rnd 2 for pattern.
Sssk (slip, slip, slip, knit) [Slip 1 st knitwise] 3 times, knit 3 sts tog through the back loop—2 st, dec.
K3tog Knit 3 sts tog—2 st dec.
I-cord With dpns, cast on designated number of sts or continue working with rem sts. *Knit one row. Without turning the work, slip the sts back to the beginning of the row. Pull the yarn tightly from the end of the row. Rep from the * as desired. Bind off.

HAT

With B, cast on 36 (44, 48, 52, 54) sts. Join, being careful not to twist sts, and pm for beg of rnd. Work 2 rnds in Seed st.

Shape muzzle

Note Muzzle is worked back and forth in rows.
Row 1 (RS) Work 14 sts in B. Change to A and work to end of rnd, turn.
Row 2 (WS) Work 22 (30, 34, 38, 40) sts in A, work 14 in B, turn.
Rows 3–8 Rep rows 1–2.
Row 9 With B, ssk, work 10, k2tog, change to B, kfb, work 20 (28, 32, 36, 38), kfb.
Row 10 With A, work 24 (32, 36, 40, 42), change to B and work 12.
Row 11 With B, ssk, work 8, k2tog, change to B, kfb, work 22 (30, 34, 38, 40), kfb.
Row 12 With A, work 26 (34, 38, 42, 44), change to B and work 10.
Row 13 With B, ssk, work 6, k2tog, change to B, kfb, work 24 (32, 36, 40, 42), kfb.
Row 14 With A, work 28 (36, 40, 44, 46), change to B and work 8.
Row 15 With B, work 8, change to A, work 28 (36, 40, 44, 46).
Row 16 With A, work 28 (36, 40, 44, 46), change to B, work 8.
Change to A, cut B, join, pm for beg of rnd.
Work even in Seed st in the rnd until hat measures 4½ (5½, 6½, 7, 7)"/11.5 (14, 16.5, 18, 18)cm from cast-on edge.

Shape crown

Rnd 1 [Work 4 (2, 4, 2, 4) sts, k2tog] 6 (11, 8, 13, 9) times—30 (33, 40, 39, 45) sts.
Rnd 2 [Work 3 (1, 3, 1, 3) sts, k2tog] 6 (11, 8, 13, 9) times—24 (22, 32, 26, 36) sts.
Rnd 3 [Work 2 (0, 2, 0, 2) sts, k2tog] 6 (11, 8, 13, 9) times—18 (11, 24, 13, 27) sts.

Sizes newborn (1–2 yrs, 6–10 yrs) ONLY

Rnd 4 [Work 1 st, k2tog] 6 (8, 9) times—12 (16, 18) sts.
Rnd 5 K2tog around—6 (8, 9) sts.

Sizes 6–12 mo (3–5 yrs) ONLY

Rnd 4 K2tog 5 (6) times, k1—6 (7) sts.

All sizes

Cut yarn, leaving a long tail, weave through rem sts, pull closed and secure end.

Magical Moose Cap

Ear flaps

Mark placement of earflaps on cast on edge. With RS facing, pick up and knit 12 sts at marker.
Rows 1–9 Work in seed st.
Row 10 (RS) K1, ssk, work 6, k2tog, k1—10 sts.
Row 11 Work even in seed st.
Rows 12–17 Rep rows 10–11—4 sts.
With dpns, work 16"/40.5cm I-cord, bind off.

MOOSE EARS (MAKE 2)
Back

With A and dpns, cast on 6 sts. Join, being careful not to twist sts, and pm for beg of rnd.
Rnd 1 and all WS rows Knit.
Rnd 2 (RS) [Kfb, k1, kfb] 2 times—10 sts.
Rnd 4 K5, kfb, k3, kfb—12 sts.
Rnd 6 Kfb, k3, kfb, kfb, k5, kfb—16 sts.
Rnd 8 Ssk, k3, k2tog, ssk, k5, k2tog—12 sts.
Rnd 10 Ssk, k1, k2tog, sssk, k1, k3tog—6 sts.
Graft sts.

Front

With B, cast on 2 sts.
Row 1, 3, 5 Purl.
Row 2 Kfb, kfb—4 sts.
Row 4 Ssk, k2tog—2 sts.
Bind Off.

ANTLERS (MAKE 2)

With B, cast on 5 sts. Work 4 rows in St st.
Cast on 4 sts at beg of next 2 rows—13 sts.
Work 2 rows even in St st.
Bind off 4 sts at beg of next 2 rows—5 sts.
Work 6 rows even in St st.
Cast on 6 sts at beg of next 2 rows—17 sts.
Inc Row (RS) Kfb, k15, kfb—19 sts.
Purl 1 row.
Dec Row (RS) Ssk, k15, k2tog—17 sts.
Purl 1 row. Bind off.

FINISHING

Seam antler, leaving the bottom open. Use tweezers to stuff antler lightly and mold into shape. Curl ends of pipe cleaner to prevent poking and insert into main antler. Sew antlers to hat at top center. Sew front of ear to lower front edge of back ear. Sew ears in place on either side of antlers. Make 2 pompoms, attach to ends of I-cords. Sew buttons on for eyes. With black embroidery floss, make 2 French knots for nostrils. ◼

Fairy House

Yarn

Lion Brand® Yarns *Vanna's Choice® Prints, Tweeds & Heathers*, 3oz/85g balls, each approx 145yd/133m (acrylic/rayon)
- 1 (1, 1, 1, 2) balls in Wheat #402 (A)
- 1 ball in Grey Marble #401 (B)

Lion Brand® Yarns *Vanna's Choice® Solids*, 3½oz/100g balls, each approx 170yd/156m (acrylic)
- 1 ball in Fern #171 (C)
- 1 ball in Silver Blue #105 (D)

Lion Brand® Yarns *Vanna's Glamour®* 1¾oz/50g balls, each approx 202yd/185m (acrylic/metallic polyester)
- 1 ball in Ruby Red #861 (E)

Lion Brand® Yarns *Sock Ease™*, 3½oz/100g balls, each approx 438yd/400m (wool/nylon)
- 1 ball in Cotton Candy #205 (F)
- 1 ball in Lemon #204 (G)

Lion Brand® Yarns *Fun Fur®*, 1¾oz/50g balls, each approx 64yd/58m (polyester)
- 1 ball in Lime #194 (H)

Needles
- One size 9 (5.5mm) circular needle, 16"/40.5cm long *or size to obtain gauge*
- One set (4) size 8 (5mm) double-pointed needles (dpns)
- One set (4) size 3 (3.25mm) double-pointed needles (dpns)

Notions
- Stitch markers
- Tapestry needle

SIZES
Newborn (6–12 mos, 1–2 yrs, 3–5 yrs, 6–10 yrs)

FINISHED MEASUREMENTS
Circumference 11 (14¾, 16½, 17¼, 18¾)"/28 (37.5, 42, 44, 47.5)cm

GAUGE
17¼ sts and 22½ rnds = 4"/10cm in St st with circular needle and A.
Take time to check your gauge.

NOTES
1 Choose hat size with circumference 2–2¾"/ 5–7cm smaller than actual head circumference.
2 Change to dpns when hat circumference gets too small for circulars. House fixtures and flowers are worked separately and sewn in place.

STITCH GLOSSARY
Garter St Knit 1 rnd, purl 1 rnd.
I-cord With dpns, cast on designated number of sts or continue working with rem sts. *Knit one row. Without turning the work, slip the sts back to the beginning of the row. Pull the yarn tightly from the end of the row. Rep from the * as desired. Bind off.

Fairy House

HAT

With H and circular needle, cast on 48 (64, 72, 78, 80) sts. Join, being careful not to twist sts, and pm for beg of rnd.
Work 4 rnds in garter st.
Change to A, work 9 (13, 15, 16, 17) rnds in St st.

Size 3–5 yrs ONLY

Next Rnd [K17, k2tog] 6 times—72 sts.

All sizes

Begin roof and shape crown
Rnd 1 Join B and work in 2 colors as foll: [k1B, k10 (14, 16, 16, 18)A, k1B] 4 times.
Rnd 2 [P1B, k1B, k8 (12, 14, 14, 16)A, k1B, p1B] 4 times.
Rnd 3 [K1B, p1B, k1B, k6 (10, 12, 12, 14)A, k1B, p1B, k1B] 4 times.
Rnd 4 [K2B, p1B, k1B, k4 (8, 10, 10, 12)A, k1B, p1B, k2B] 4 times.
Rnd 5 [P1B, k2B, p1B, k1B, k2 (6, 8, 8, 10)A, k1B, p1B, k2B, p1B] 4 times.
Rnd 6 [SspB, k2B, p1B, k1B, K0 (4, 6, 6, 8)A, k1B, p1B, k2B, p2togB] 4 times—40 (56, 64, 64, 72) sts.

Size newborn ONLY

Rnd 7 Cut A, with B, [k1, p1, k2, p2, k2, p1, k1] 4 times.
Rnd 8 [Ssk, p1, k4, p1, k2tog] 4 times—32 sts.
Rnd 9 [K2, p1, k2, p1, k2] 4 times.
Rnd 10 [Ssk, k1, p2, k1, k2tog] 4 times—24 sts.
Rnd 11 [P1, k4, p1] 4 times.
Rnd 12 [Ssp, k2, p2tog] 4 times—16 sts.
Rnd 13 [K1, p2, k1] 4 times.
Rnd 14 [Ssk, k2tog] 4 times—8 sts.
Rnd 15 [K2tog] 4 times—4 sts.

Size 6–12 mos ONLY

Rnd 7 [(K1, p1, k2, p1, k1)B, k2A, (k1, p1, k2, p1, k1)B] 4 times.
Rnd 8 Cut A, with B, [ssk, p1, k2, p1, k2, p1, k2, k2tog] 4 times—48 sts.
Rnd 9 [K2, p1, k2, p2, k2, p1, k2] 4 times.
Rnd 10 [Ssk, k1, p1, k4, p1, k1, k2tog] 4 times—40 sts.
Rnd 11 [P1, k2, p1, k2, p1, k2, p1] 4 times.
Rnd 12 [Ssp, k2, p2, k2, p2tog] 4 times—32 sts.
Rnd 13 [K1, p1, k4, p1, k1] 4 times.
Rnd 14 [Ssk, p1, k2, p1, k2tog] 4 times—24 sts.
Rnd 15 [K2, p2, k2] 4 times.
Rnd 16 [Ssk, k2, k2tog] 4 times—16 sts.
Rnd 17 [P1, k2, p1] 4 times.
Rnd 18 [Ssp, p2tog] 4 times—8 sts.
Rnd 19 [K2tog] 4 times—4 sts.

Sizes 1–2 yrs (3–5 yrs) ONLY

Rnd 7 [(K1, p1, k2, p1, k1)B, k4A, (k1, p1, k2, p1, k1)B] 4 times.
Rnd 8 [(Ssk, p1, k2, p1, k1)B, k2A, (k1, p1, k2, p1, k2tog)B] 4 times—56 sts.
Rnd 9 Cut A, with B, [k2, p1, k2, p1, k2, p1, k2] 4 times.
Rnd 10 [Ssk, k1, p1, k2, p2, k2, p1, k1, k2tog] 4 times—48 sts.
Rnd 11 [P1, k2, p1, k4, p1, k2, p1] 4 times.
Rnd 12 [Ssp, k2, p1, k2, p1, k2, p2tog] 4 times—40 sts.
Rnd 13 [K1, p1, k2, p2, k2, p1, k1] 4 times.
Rnds 14–21 Rep rows 8–15 of Newborn Size.

Size 6–10 yrs ONLY

Rnd 7 [(K1, p1, k2, p1, k1)B, k6A, (k1, p1, k2, p1, k1)B] 4 times.
Rnd 8 [(Ssk, p1, k2, p1, k1)B, k4A, (k1, p1, k2, p1, k2tog)B] 4 times—64 sts.
Rnd 9 [(K2, p1, k2, p1, k1)B, k2A, (k1, p1, k2, p1, k2)B] 4 times.
Rnd 10 Cut A, with B, [ssk, k1, p1, k2, p1, k2, p1, k1, k2tog] 4 times—56 sts.
Rnd 11 [P1, k2, p1, k2, p1, k2, p1, k2, p1] 4 times.
Rnd 12 [Ssp, k2, p1, k4, p1, k2, p2tog] 4 times—48 sts.
Rnd 13 [K1, p1, k2, p1, k4, p1, k2, p1, k1] 4 times.
Rnd 14 [Ssk, p1, k2, p2, k2, p1, p2tog] 4 times—40 sts.
Rnd 15 [K2, p1, k4, p1, k2] 4 times.
Rnd 16 [Ssk, k1, p1, k2, p1, k1, k2tog] 4 times—32 sts.
Rnd 17 [P1, k2, p2, k2, p1] 4 times.
Rnd 18 [Ssp, k4, p2tog] 4 times—24 sts.
Rnd 19 [K1, p1, k2, p2, k1] 4 times.
Rnd 20 [Ssk, p2, k2tog] 4 times—16 sts.
Rnd 21 Knit.
Rnd 22 [Ssp, p2tog] 4 times—8 sts.
Rnd 23 K2tog 4 times—4 sts.

All sizes

Work 2 rows of I-cord, fasten off.

Door

With E and larger dpns, cast on 14. Work 12 rows in St st. bind off 2 sts at beg of next 4 rows. Bind off rem 6 sts.

Chimney

With E and larger dpns, cast on 5 sts. Work 6 rows of I-cord, bind off.

Windows (make 3)

With D and larger dpns, cast on 7 sts. Work 7 rows in St st. Bind off on next WS row.

Flower A (make 6)

With F and smaller dpns, cast on 4 sts, bind off 3 sts, [slide last st over to the left needle. Use knitted cast-on and cast on 3 sts, bind off 3 sts] 4 times. Fasten off, use tail to gather petals together in center. Use G and embroider a French knot in center.

Flower B (make 6)

With G and smaller dpns, cast on 16 sts. Work 4 rows in St st.
Next Row [K2tog] 8 times—8 sts.
Cut yarn, leaving a long tail, weave through rem sts, pull closed with WS facing out and the edges tuck into the center. Sew side seam. With F, embroider a French knot in center.

FINISHING

With C, using (3) 16"/40.5 cm strands for each cord, make 2 twisted cords and attach to sides of hat. Make 2 tassels and attach to end of twisted cords. Sew twisted cord to sides of hat. Sew door to one side of hat, slightly to the left of twisted cord placement. With G, embroider a French knot for the door knob. Sew chimney to top of roof, over the door. Sew windows around sides of hat, just under the roof. Use E and embroider window panes into place around windows, as pictured. Sew flowers around door, windows, grass. ■

Raccoon Cape

Yarn 5 6

Lion Brand® Yarns *Jiffy®*, 3oz/85g balls, each approx 135yd/123m (acrylic)
- 1 (2, 2, 2) balls in Dark Grey Heather #159 (A)
- 1 (2, 2, 2) balls in Black #153 (B)
- 1 ball in White #100 (C)
- 1 ball in Silver Heather #155 (D)

Lion Brand® Yarns *Luxe Fur*, 1¾oz/50g balls, each approx 44yd/40m (wool/acrylic/nylon)
- 2 balls in Ash #150 (E)

Needles

- One size 10 (6mm) circular needle, 24"/61cm long *or size to obtain gauge*
- One size 11 (5.5mm) circular needle, 40"/101.5cm long

Notions

- Stitch markers
- Tapestry needle
- 2 Black shank buttons ½"/1.5cm in diameter
- 1 Black velvet button ⅝"/1.5cm in diameter

SIZES

1–2 yrs (3–5 yrs, 6–10 yrs)

FINISHED MEASUREMENTS

Width at lower edge (above ruffle) 29½ (29½, 32¾)"/74 (74, 83)cm

Length from lower edge to shoulder (excluding ruffle) 11"/28cm

GAUGE

15 sts and 19 rows = 4"/10cm in St st with smaller needles.
Take time to check your gauge.

NOTES

1 When changing colors, twist yarns on WS to prevent holes in work.
2 Use a separate bobbin for each color section when working Raccoon Chart. Do not carry yarn across back of work.

CAPE

With B and smaller needles, cast on 111 (111, 123) sts.

Beg Chevron Chart

Row 1 (RS) Work to rep line, work 12-st rep 9 (9, 10) times across, work to end of chart.
Cont to work chart in this way through row 40. Then rep rows 1–10 once more.

Shape hood

Cont with A only, work 6 rows in St st.

Size 1–2 yrs ONLY

Row 1 (RS) *[K2, k2tog] 2 times, k1,k2tog. Rep from * 9 times more, k1—81 sts.
Row 2 (WS) *[P1, p2tog] 3 times, p2tog. Rep from * 6 times more, p1, p2tog, p1—52 sts.

Size 3–5 yrs ONLY

Row 1 (RS) [K2, k2tog] 27 times, k1, k2tog—83 sts.
Row 2 (WS) [P1, p2tog] 27 times, p2—56 sts.

Size 6–10 yrs ONLY

Row 1 (RS) *[K2, k2tog] 5 times, k1, k2tog. Rep from * 4 times more, [k2, k2tog] 2 times—91 sts.
Row 2 (WS) [P1, p2tog] 30 times, p1—61 sts.

All sizes

Row 3 Knit.
Row 4 K1, p50 (54, 59), k1.
Rep last 2 rows 2 (4, 4) times more.

Beg Raccoon Chart

Next row (RS) K6 (8, 10), work Raccoon Chart, k5 (7, 10).
Next row (WS) K1, p4 (6, 9), work Raccoon Chart, p5 (7, 9), k1.
Cont to work Raccoon Chart in this way through row 32. Cut B and C, cont with A only.
Work 12 (10, 12) rows even in St st.
Divide sts evenly on 2 needles and graft to close hood.

Trim

With E and larger needles, begin at bottom corner with RS facing, pick up and knit 100 (102, 104) sts evenly spaced along front opening and 109 (109, 121) sts along bottom edge. Join, pm for beg of rnd—209 (211, 225) sts.
Rnd 1 P1, pfb, p96, pfb, p2, pfb, p105 (107, 121), pfb, p1—213 (215, 229) sts.
Rnds 2 and 4 Knit.
Rnd 3 P1, pfb, 98, pfb, p2, pfb, p107 (109, 123), pfb, p1—217 (219, 233) sts.
Rnd 5 [P1, pfb] to last st, p1—325 (328, 349) sts.
Bind off.

FINISHING

Sew shank buttons to inner corner of eyes and velvet button to nose.
Split a 12"/30.5cm length of black yarn into two 2-ply strands. Embroider a smile at bottom edge of face. ■

Raccoon Cape

RACCOON CHART

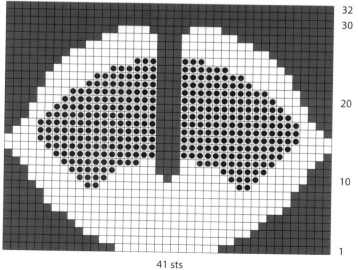

32
30

20

10

1

41 sts

COLOR KEY

- ■ Color A
- ◉ Color B
- □ Color C
- ▥ Color D

CHEVRON CHART

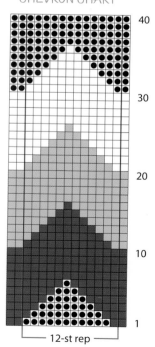

40

30

20

10

1

12-st rep

Squirrel Set

Yarn ④ ③

Red Heart® *Shimmer*™, 3½oz/100g balls, each approx 280yd/256m (acrylic/metallic polyester)
- 1 (1, 2, 2, 2) balls in Lime #1625 (A)

Red Heart® *Sport*, 2½oz / 70g skeins, each approx 165yd/150m (acrylic)
- 1 skein in Wood Brown #361 (B)
- 1 skein in Fawn #322 (C)

Needles

- One size 8 (5mm) circular needle, 16"/40.5cm long
- One size 9 (5.5mm) circular needle, 16"/40.5cm long *or size to obtain gauge*
- One set (4) size 9 (5.5mm) double-pointed needles (dpns)
- One pair size 4 (3.5mm) needles
- One pair size 3 (3.25mm) double-pointed needles (dpns)

Notions

- Stitch marker
- Tapestry needle
- 3 black seed beads, needle and matching thread
- Approx 1yd/1m of ⅝"/1.5cm wide gingham ribbon
- Stuffing
- Hairbrush

SIZES

Hat Newborn (6–12 mos, 1–2 yrs, 3–5 yrs, 6–10 yrs)
Cowl One size

FINISHED MEASUREMENTS

Hat circumference 12 (15, 18, 18, 19½)"/30.5 (38, 45.5, 45.5, 49.5)cm
Cowl length 23¼"/59cm

GAUGE

16 sts and 22 rnds = 4"/10cm in St st with larger circular needle and 2 strands of A held together.
Take time to check your gauge.

NOTES

1 Choose hat size with circumference 1½–2"/4–5cm smaller than actual head circumference.
2 The circumference is the same for 1–2 yrs and 3–5 yrs, the hat length is approx. ¾"/2cm longer for the larger size.
3 Squirrel and acorns are worked separately and sewn in place.

STITCH GLOSSARY

K3, p3 rib
Rnd 1 [K3, p3] around.
Rnd 2 Knit the knits and purl the purls.
Rep rnd 2 for pattern.
Sssk (slip, slip, slip, knit) [Slip 1 st knitwise] 3 times, knit 3 sts tog through the back loops— 2 sts dec.

Squirrel Set

K3tog Knit 3 stitches together—2 sts dec.

I-cord With dpns, cast on designated number of sts or continue working with rem sts. *Knit one row. Without turning the work, slip the sts back to the beginning of the row. Pull the yarn tightly from the end of the row. Rep from the * as desired. Bind off.

HAT

With 2 strands of A and smaller circular needle, cast on 48 (60, 72, 72, 78) sts. Join, being careful not to twist sts, and pm for beg of rnd.

Work 6 rnds in K3, p3 rib. Change to larger circular needle.

[Purl 8 rnds, knit 4 rnds] for welt pattern until hat measures 4¾ (6¼, 6½, 7¼, 7¾)"/12 (16, 16.5, 18.5, 19.5)cm from cast-on edge.

Shape crown

Note Maintain welt pattern; use p2tog to dec on purl rnds and k2tog to dec on knit rnds.

Rnd 1 [Work 4, dec 1] around—40 (50, 60, 60, 65) sts.

Rnds 2 and 4 Work even.

Rnd 3 [Work 3, dec 1] around—32 (40, 48, 48, 52) sts.

Rnd 5 [Work 2, dec 1] around—24 (30, 36, 36, 39) sts.

Rnd 6 [Work 1, dec 1] around—16 (20, 24, 24, 26) sts.

Rnd 7 *Dec 1. Rep from * around—8 (10, 12, 12, 13) sts.

Rnd 8 Rep rnd 7—4 (5, 6, 6, 7) sts.

Cut yarn leaving a long tail, weave through rem sts, pull closed and secure end.

COWL

With 2 strands of A and larger circular needle, cast on 93 sts. Join, being careful not to twist sts, and pm for beg of rnd.

Work 6 rnds even in k3, p3 rib. Change to St st and work until cowl measures 4¼"/11cm from cast-on edge, ending with a RS row.

Eyelet row (WS) K1, p2, [yo, p2tog, p6] 11 times, p1, k1.

Knit 4 rows. Bind off.

SQUIRREL

Body

With B and straight needles, cast on 4 sts.

Row 1 (RS) Purl.

Row 2 (WS) [Kfb] 4 times—8 sts.

Row 3 [Kfb] 3 times, k2, [kfb] 3 times—14 sts.

Rows 4–10, Work even in St st.

Row 11 K1, ssk, knit to last 3 sts, k2tog, k1—12 sts.

Row 12 Purl

Row 13–16 Rep rows 11–12 twice—8 sts.

Row 17 K1, sssk, k3tog, k1—4 sts. Bind off.

With smallest needles, pick up and knit 2 sts from front of body for front leg, work 3 row I-cord, bind off. Slightly tuck I-cord, and sew end in place. Rep for 2nd leg.

Head

With B and straight needles, cast on 4 sts. Rep rows 1–4 of body.

Row 5 K4, kfb, turn, p3, turn, k2tog, k6, kfb, turn, p3, turn, k2tog, k4.

Rows 6–8 Work even in St st.

Row 9 K4, ssk, k2, k2tog, k4—12 sts.

Rows 10 and 12 Purl.

Row 11 K1, [ssk] 2 times, k2, [k2tog] 2 times, k1—8 sts.

Row 13 K1, k2tog 2 times, k1—5 sts.

Cut yarn leaving a long tail, weave through rem sts, pull closed and secure end.

Tail

With B and smallest needles, cast on 6 sts.

Row 1 (RS) K1, kfb, k5, kfb, k1—8 sts.

Rows 2, 4 and 14 Purl.

Row 3 [K1, kfb] 4 times—12 sts.

Row 5 [K1, kfb] 2 times, k4, [kfb, k1] 2 times—16 sts.

Rows 7–12 Work even in St st.

Row 13 [K1, k2tog] 2 times, k4, [k2tog, k1] 2 times—12 sts.

Row 15 K1, k2tog 5 times, k1—7 sts. Bind off.

Sew back seams of squirrel body and head, leaving small openings. Stuff body and head into shape. Sew openings; sew head to body. Using a thick bristle brush (a pet hair brush works great), brush tail until soft and fuzzy. Sew onto rear of squirrel.

ACORNS

Large acorn

With C and smallest needles, cast on 6 sts.

Rows 1, 3, 5, 7, 8 and 10 (WS) Purl.

Row 2 (RS) K1, [kfb] 4 times, k1—10 sts.

Row 4 K1, [kfb, k2] 3 times—13 sts.

Row 6 Knit. Cut C and change to B.

Row 9 Knit.

Row 11 K1, [k2tog] 6 times—7 sts.

Row 12 K1, ssk, k3tog, k1—4 sts. Do not turn. Work 3 row I-cord, bind off.

Small acorns (make 2)

With C and smallest needles, cast on 6 sts.

Rows 1, 3, 5, 6 and 8 (WS) Purl.

Row 2 (RS) K1, [kfb] 4 times, k1—10 sts.

Row 4 Knit. Cut C and change to B.

Row 7 Knit.

Row 9 K1, k2tog 4 times, k1—6 sts.

Row 10 Sssk, k3tog—2 sts. Do not turn. Work 3 row I-cord, bind off.

Lightly stuff acorns and sew up the seams. Sew large acorn and squirrel onto hat, as desired. Weave ribbon through eyelets on cowl. Tie cowl closed as desired. Sew small acorns to ends of ribbon. ■

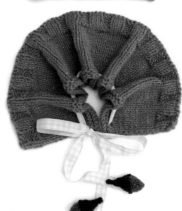

Ladybug Hat + Cape

Yarn 4

Bernat® *Sheep(ish)* by Vickie Howell, 3oz/85g balls, each approx 167yd/153m (acrylic/wool)
- 2 (2, 2, 2, 3) balls in Red(ish) #15 (A)
- 1 ball in Chartreuse(ish) #20 (B)
- Small amount of worsted weight black yarn (C)

Needles

- One size 8 (5mm) circular needle, 16"/40.5cm long *or size to obtain gauge*
- One set (4) size 8 (5mm) double-pointed needles (dpns)

Notions

- Stitch markers
- Tapestry needle
- ⅞"/2cm wide ribbon approx 2yd/2m long

SIZES

Hat Newborn (6–12 mos, 1–2 yrs, 3–5 yrs, 6–10 yrs)
Scarf One size

FINISHED MEASUREMENTS

Hat circumference 12 (15½, 17¼, 18¼, 19½)"/30.5 (39.5, 44, 46.5, 49.5)cm
Scarf length 40"/101.5cm

GAUGE

18½ sts and 24 rows = 4"/10cm in St st with size 8 (5mm) needles.
Take time to check your gauge.

NOTES

1 Choose hat size with circumference 1–2"/2.5–5cm smaller than actual head circumference.
2 Change to dpns when hat circumference gets too small for circular.

STITCH GLOSSARY

K-tbl, p1 rib (over an even number of sts)
Rnd 1 [Knit 1 through back loop, p1] around.
Rnd 2 K-tbl in the knit sts and purl the purls.
Rep rnd 2 for pattern.
S2KP Slip 2, knit 1, pass slipped sts over—2 sts dec.

I-cord With dpns, cast on designated number sts or continue working with rem sts. *Knit one row. Without turning the work, slip the sts back to the beginning of the row. Pull the yarn tightly from the end of the row. Rep from the * as desired. Bind off.

HAT

With A, cast on 56 (72, 80, 84, 90) sts. Join, being careful not to twist sts, and pm for beg of rnd.
Work 6 rnds K-tbl, p1 rib.
Work in St st until work measures 6¾ (8, 8¼, 9, 9¼)"/17 (20.5, 21, 23, 23.5)cm from cast-on edge.

Shape crown

Rnd 1 [K2 (4, 3, 4, 4), k2tog] 14 (12, 16, 14, 15) times—42 (60, 64, 70, 75) sts.
Rnd 2 [K1 (3, 2, 3, 3), k2tog] 14 (12, 16, 14, 15) times—28 (48, 48, 56, 60) sts.
Rnd 3 [K0 (2, 1, 2, 2), k2tog] 14 (12, 16, 14, 15) times—14 (36, 32, 42, 45) sts.

Sizes 6–12 mos (1–2yrs, 3–5 yrs, 6–10 yrs) ONLY
Rnd 4 [K1 (0, 1, 1), k2tog] 12 (16, 14, 15) times—24 (16, 28, 30) sts.

All sizes
Next rnd [K2tog] 7 (12, 16, 14, 15) times—7 (12, 16, 14, 15) sts.

Sizes 6–12 mos (1–2 yrs, 3–5 yrs) ONLY
Next rnd [K2tog] 6 (8, 7) times—6 (8, 7) sts.

Size 6–10 yrs ONLY
Next rnd [K2tog] 7 times, k1—8 sts.
Cut yarn leaving a long tail, weave through rem sts, pull closed and secure end.

SCARF

With A, cast on 24 sts. Knit 4 rows. Work 2 rows in St st.
Eyelet Row (RS) K3, k2tog, yo, k19.
Continue in St st and rep eyelet row every 12th row until scarf measures 39"/99cm from cast-on edge, ending with a WS row. Knit 4 rows, bind off.
With bottom RS edge facing, pick up 180 sts evenly spaced across.
Inc row (WS) Pfb across—360 sts.
Work 7 rows in St st. Knit 1 row, bind off.
With top RS edge facing, with B, pick up 180 sts evenly spaced across. Knit 3 rows, bind off.

LADYBUG

With A, cast on 7 sts. Do not turn (work like an I-cord).
Row 1 (RS) Knit.
Rows 2, 4 and 6 (WS) K1, kfb, k3, kfb, k1—inc 2 sts.
Rows 3, 5, 7 and 8 Knit.
Row 9 K6, join C, k1C, k6A.
Row 10 K6A, k1C, k6A.
Row 11 (Ssk, k4)A, k1C, (k4, k2tog)A—11 sts.
Row 12 (Ssk, k2)A, k3C, (k2, k2tog)A—9 sts.
Row 13 Cut A, with C, ssk, k5, k2tog—7 sts.
Row 14 Ssk, k3, k2tog—5 sts.
Row 15 Ssk, k1, k2tog—3 sts. Bind off.

LEAF

With B, cast on 3 sts. Work 4 rows I-cord. Begin working in rows as follows:
working in St st, cast on 2 sts at beg of next 2 rows—7 sts.
Cast on 3 sts at beg of next 2 rows—13 sts.
Work 4 rows even in St st.
Row 1 (RS) K1, ssk, knit to last 3 sts, k2tog, k1—dec 2 sts.
Row 2 K1, purl to last st, k1.
Rows 3–8 Rep last 2 rows.
Row 9 K1, S2KP, k1—3 sts.
Row 10 S2KP—1 st. Fasten off.

FINISHING

Using C, embroider 4–5 french knots onto ladybug wings. Sew leaf to side of hat. Sew ladybug to sit slightly on top of leaf. Block ribbon to enhance ruffles, if desired. Weave ribbon through eyelets of scarf and tie in a bow. ■

Bee Sweet

Yarn 4

Lion Brand® Yarns *Vanna's Choice® Solids*,
3½oz/100g balls, each approx 170yd/156m (acrylic)
- 1 (1, 1, 1, 2) balls in Mustard #158 (A)
- 1 ball in Black #153 (B)
- 1 ball in White #100 (C)

Lion Brand® Yarns *Vanna's Choice® Baby*,
3½oz/100g balls, each approx 170yd/156m (acrylic)
- 1 ball in Ducky #157 (D)

Needles

- One size 9 (5.5mm) circular needle,
  16"/40.5cm long *or size to obtain gauge*
- One set (4) size 9 (5.5mm)
  double-pointed needles (dpns)
- One set (4) size 7 (4.5mm)
  double-pointed needles (dpns)

Notions
- Stitch markers
- Tapestry needle
- Stuffing
- Tweezers

SIZES
Hat Newborn (6–12 mos, 1–2 yrs, 3–5 yrs, 6–10 yrs)
Mitt 6–12 mos (1–2 yrs, 3–5 yrs, 6–10 yrs)

FINISHED MEASUREMENTS
Hat circumference 11 (14¾, 16½, 17¼,
18¾)"/28 (37.5, 42, 44, 47.5)cm
Mitt circumference 4½ (5¼, 5¾, 6½)"/11.5
(13.5, 14.5, 16.5)cm

GAUGE
17¼ sts and 22½ rows = 4"/10 cm in St st
with larger needles and A.
Take time to check your gauge.

NOTES
1 Choose hat size with circumference 2–2¾"/5–
  7cm smaller than actual head circumference.
2 Decreases (Dec 1) are worked as p2tog in purl
  rnds and k2tog in knit rnds.
3 Change to dpns when hat circumference gets too
  small for circular.
4 Bees are worked separately and sewn in place.

STITCH GLOSSARY
K1, p1 rib (over an even number of sts)
Rnd 1 [K1, p1] around.
Rnd 2 Knit the knits and purl the purls.
Rep rnd 2 for pattern.

I-cord With dpns, cast on designated number
of sts or continue working with rem sts. *Knit
one row. Without turning the work, slip the sts
back to the beginning of the row. Pull the yarn
tightly from the end of the row. Rep from the *
as desired. Bind off.

HAT
With A and larger needles, cast on 48 (64, 72, 78,
80) sts. Join, being careful not to twist sts, and pm
for beg of rnd.
Knit 7 rnds.
[Purl 6 rnds, knit 3 rnds] for welt pattern until work
measures 4 (5¾, 6, 6½, 7)"/10 (14.5, 16.5, 18)cm
from beg.

Shape crown
Maintain welt pattern as established.
Rnd 1 [Work 6 (6, 6, 4, 6) sts, dec 1] 6 (8, 9, 13, 10)
times—42 (56, 63, 65, 70) sts.
Rnds 2 and 4 Work even in pattern.
Rnd 3 [Work 5 (5, 5, 3, 5) sts, dec 1] 6 (8, 9, 13, 10)
times—36 (48, 54, 52, 60) sts.
Rnd 5 [Work 4 (4, 4, 2, 4) sts, dec 1] 6 (8, 9, 13, 10)
times—30 (40, 45, 39, 50) sts.

*Sizes newborn (6–12 mos, 1–2 yrs,
6–10 yrs) ONLY*
Rnd 6 [Work 3 sts, dec 1] 6 (8, 9, 10) times—24
(32, 36, 40) sts.
Rnd 7 [Work 2 sts, dec 1] 6 (8, 9, 10) times—18
(24, 27, 30) sts.
Rnd 8 [Work 1 st, dec 1] 6 (8, 9, 10) times—12
(16, 18, 20) sts.
Rnd 9 [Dec 1] 6 (8, 9, 10) times—6 (8, 9, 10) sts.

Sizes 1–2 yrs (6–10 yrs) ONLY
Rnd 10 [Dec 1] 4 (5) times, work 1 (0) —5 sts.

Size 3–5 yrs ONLY
Rnds 6 and 8 Work even in patt.
Rnd 7 [Work 1, dec 1] 13 times—26 sts.
Rnd 9 [Dec 1] 13 times—13 sts.
Rnd 10 [Dec 1] 6 times, work 1—7 sts.
Cut yarn leaving a long tail, weave through rem sts,
pull closed and secure end.

MITTS
With A and smaller dpns, cast on 20 (22, 24, 28) sts.
Join, being careful not to twist sts, and pm for beg
of rnd.
Knit 7 rnds.
[Purl 6 rnds, knit 3 rnds] for welt pattern 3 times.
Change to K1, p1 rib and work 7 (7, 10, 12)
rnds even.
Beg working in rows for thumb opening.
Work 4 (6, 6, 8) rows in ribbing as established.
Join to work in rnds, pm for beg of rnd.
Work 6 (6, 8, 10) rnds in rib as established, bind off.

BEES (MAKE 4)
Body
With B and smaller needles, cast on 5 sts.
Row 1 (RS) [Kfb] 5 times—10 sts.
Row 2 (WS) Change to D, purl.
Row 3 K1, kfb, knit 6, kfb, k1—12 sts.
Row 4 Change to B, purl.
Row 5 Knit.
Row 6 Change to D, purl.
Row 7 K1, ssk, knit 6, k2tog, k1—10 sts.
Row 8 Change to B, purl.
Row 9 K1, k3tog, k2tog, k3tog, k1—5 sts.
Row 10 P2tog, p1, p2tog. Cut yarn leaving a
long tail, weave through rem sts, pull closed and
secure end.

Wings
With C and smaller needles, cast on 2 sts. Work 20
rows I-cord, bind off.

FINISHING
Sew back seam of bee, leaving a small opening. Use
tweezers to lightly stuff the bees, finish seam. Fold
I-cord into Figure 8 shape, pinch the center and sew
to top of bees.
Sew 3 bees onto hat, as desired. Sew one bee on
each mitt, as desired. ■

Funny Fox

Yarn

Lion Brand® Yarns *Jiffy®*, 3oz/85g balls, each approx 135yd/123m (acrylic)
- 1 (1, 1, 2, 2) balls in Chili #115 (A)
- 1 ball in White #100 (B)
- 1 ball in Silver Heather #155 (C)

Needles

- One size 15 (10mm) circular needle, 24"/61cm long *or size to obtain gauge*

Notions

- Stitch markers
- Tapestry needle
- 1 Velvet shank button ⅝"/1.5cm in diameter
- 3 Black buttons ⅞"/2cm in diameter
- Stuffing

SIZES
Newborn (6–12 mos, 1–2 yrs, 3–5 yrs, 6–10 yrs)

FINISHED MEASUREMENTS
Circumference 10½ (14½, 16, 16¾, 18½)"/26.5 (37, 40.5, 42.5, 47)cm

GAUGE
10 sts and 14 rows = 4"/10cm in St st with 2 strands of A.
Take time to check your gauge.

NOTES
1 Choose hat size with circumference 2½–3"/6.5–7.5 cm smaller than actual head circumference.
2 Piece is worked with 2 strands of yarn held together throughout.
3 The cowl is worked in the rnd. When length is reached, hood is worked in rows.
4 The ears are made separately and sewn in place.

STITCH GLOSSARY
Garter st Knit 1 rnd, purl 1 rnd.
S2KP Slip 2, knit 1, pass slipped sts over—2 st dec.

COWL
With 2 strands of B, cast on 38 (42, 46, 50, 56) sts. Join, being careful not to twist sts, and pm for beg of rnd.

Work 4 rnds in garter st.
Change to C, work 5 rnds in St st.
Change to A, work in St st (k every rnd) until cowl measures 5 (5¼, 5½, 5¾, 6)"/12.5 (13.5, 14, 14.5, 15)cm from cast-on edge.

Shape hood
Row 1 (RS) K1, ssk, k32 (36, 40, 44, 50), k2tog, k1—36 (40, 44, 48, 54) sts.
Row 2 (WS) K1, purl to last st, k1.
Rep last 2 rows 1 (0, 0, 1, 0) time more—34 (40, 44, 46, 54) sts.
Row 5 (3, 3, 5, 3) Bind off 2 sts at beg of row, knit to end—32 (38, 42, 44, 52) sts.
Row 6 (4, 4, 6, 4) Bind off 2 sts at beg of row, purl to last st, k1—30 (36, 40, 42, 50) sts.
Rep last 2 rows 1 (0, 0, 0, 1) time more—26 (36, 40, 42, 46) sts.
Work even in St st until hood measures 6 (6½, 6¾, 7, 7¼)"/15 (16.5, 17, 18, 18.5)cm from cowl edge, ending with a WS row.
Next row (RS) Join B, work Chart A on 1st 10 sts, drop B, k6 (16, 20, 22, 26) sts with A, join a new ball of B and work Chart B on last 10 sts.
Next row Work Chart B on 1st 10 sts, k6 (16, 20, 22, 26) sts with A, work Chart A on last 10 sts.
Rep last 2 rows until row 13 of charts is complete.
Bind off and seam the hood.

FOX EARS (MAKE 2)
Outer ear
With 2 strands of A, cast on 11 sts.
Rows 1, 3 and 9 Knit.
Row 2 (and all even rows) Purl.
Rows 5, 7 and 11 (RS) Ssk, knit to last 2 sts, k2tog—2 sts dec.
Row 13 K1, S2KP, k1—3 sts.
Purl 1 row. Bind off.

Inner ear
With 2 strands of B, cast on 9 sts.
Rows 1, 3 and 7 (RS) Knit
Row 2 (and all even rows) Purl
Rows 5, 9 Ssk, knit to last 2 sts, k2tog—2 sts dec.
Row 11 K1, S2KP, k1—3 sts.
Row 13 Knit.
Bind off.

FINISHING
Hood edging
With RS facing, 2 strands of B held tog, and at a rate of 2 sts for every 3 rows, pick up and knit an even number of stitches around hood. Join, and pm for beg of rnd. Work 4 rnds in garter st. Bind off. With RS tog, backstitch inner ear to outer ear, leaving bottom edge open. Turn RS out and stuff lightly. Sew bottom edge, cinching it to make a slightly curved shape. Sew ears to side of hood seam, allowing to point forward a bit.

Sew 3 buttons to cowl, below the hood neck. Sew velvet button to apex of white muzzle. ■

COLOR KEY

■ Color A
□ Color B

CHART A   CHART B

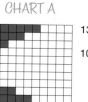
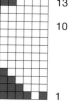
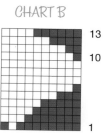

10 sts   10 sts

Froggy Hat

Yarn

Premier® Yarns Deborah Norville
Collection™ *Everyday*® Soft Worsted, 4oz/113g
balls, each approx 203yd/186m (acrylic)
• 1 (1, 1, 1, 2) balls in Shamrock #100-29 (A)
Premier® Yarns Deborah Norville Collection™
Serenity® Sock Solids, 1¾oz/28g balls,
each approx 230yd/210m (acrylic)
• 1 ball in Soft White #150-01 (B)

Needles

• One size 8 (5mm) circular needle, 16"/40.5cm
long *or size to obtain gauge*
• One set (4) size 8 (5mm)
double-pointed needles (dpns)
• One pair size 7 (4.5mm) needles
• One pair size 5 (3.75mm) needles

Notions

• Stitch markers
• Tapestry needle
• 2 Shank buttons ⅞"/2 cm in diameter
• Sewing thread and needle
• Stuffing
• Hairspray (optional)

SIZES

Newborn (6–12 mos, 1–2 yrs, 3–5 yrs, 6–10 yrs)

FINISHED MEASUREMENTS

Circumference 12½ (16, 17¾, 18¾, 19)"/32
(40.5, 45, 47.5, 48.5)cm

GAUGE

18 sts and 24 rows = 4"/10 cm in St st with
largest needles.
Take time to check your gauge.

NOTES

1 Choose hat size with circumference 1–2"/2.5–
5cm smaller than actual head circumference.
2 Change to dpns when hat circumference gets too
small for circular.
3 Froggy eyes are worked in pieces and sewn
together before sewing on hat.

STITCH GLOSSARY

K2, p2 rib (multiple of 4 sts)
Rnd 1 [K, p2] around.
Rnd 2 Knit the knits and purl the purls.
Rep rnd 2 for pattern.
I-cord With dpns, cast on designated number of
sts or continue working with rem sts. *Knit one
row. Without turning the work, slip the sts back
to the beginning of the row. Pull the yarn tightly
from the end of the row. Rep from the * as desired.
Bind off.

HAT

With B and larger needle, cast on 56 (72, 80, 84,
88) sts. Join, being careful not to twist sts, and pm
for beg of rnd.
Work 6 rnds in k2, p2 rib.
Work in St st until hat measures 4 (5¼, 5½, 5¾,
6¼)"/10 (13.5, 14, 14.5, 16)cm from cast-on edge.

Shape crown

Rnd 1 [K5 (7, 8, 10, 9) sts, k2tog] 8 (8, 8, 7, 8)
times—48 (64, 72, 77, 80) sts.
Rnd 2 [K4 (6, 7, 9, 8) sts, k2tog] 8 (8, 8, 7, 8)
times—40 (56, 64, 70, 72) sts.
Rnd 3 [K3 (5, 6, 8, 7) sts, k2tog] 8 (8, 8, 7, 8)
times—32 (48, 56, 63, 64) sts.
Rnd 4 [K2 (4, 5, 7, 6) sts, k2tog] 8 (8, 8, 7, 8)
times—24 (40, 48, 56, 56) sts.
Rnd 5 [K1 (3, 4, 6, 5) sts, k2tog] 8 (8, 8, 7, 8)
times—16 (32, 40, 49, 48) sts.
Rnd 6 [K0 (2, 3, 5, 4) sts, k2tog] 8 (8, 8, 7, 8)
times—8 (24, 32, 42, 40) sts.

Sizes 6–12 mos (1–2 yrs, 3–5 yrs,
6–10 yrs) ONLY
Rnd 7 [K1 (2, 4, 3) sts, k2tog] 8 (8, 7, 8) times—16
(24, 35, 32) sts.
Rnd 8 [K0 (1, 3, 2) sts, k2tog] 8 (8, 7, 8) times—8
(16, 28, 24) sts.

Sizes 1–2 yrs (3–5 yrs, 6–10 yrs) ONLY
Rnd 9 [K0 (2, 1) sts, k2tog] 8 (7, 8) times—8 (21,
16) sts.

Sizes 3–5 yrs (6–10 yrs) ONLY
Rnd 10 [K1 (0) sts, k2tog] 7 (8) times—14 (8) sts.

Size 3–5 yrs ONLY
Rnd 11 [K2tog] 7 times—7 sts.
Rnd 12 [K2tog] 3 times, k1—4 sts.

Sizes newborn (6–12 mos, 1–2 yrs,
6–10 yrs) ONLY
Final rnd [K2tog] 4 times—4 sts.
Cut yarn leaving a long tail, weave through rem sts,
pull closed and secure end.

Ear flaps (make 2)

Mark ear flap placement with stitch markers on
either side of the brim. With A, larger needle, and
RS facing, pick up and knit 12 (14, 14, 14, 16) sts at
marked location.
Row 1 (WS) K2, p8 (10, 10, 10, 12), k2.
Row 2 (RS) Knit.
Rep last 2 rows 6 times more. Work 1 WS row.
Dec row (RS) K2, ssk, k4 (6, 6, 6, 8), k2tog,
k2—10 (12, 12, 12, 14) sts.
Next row (WS) K2, p 6 (8, 8, 8, 10), k2.
Rep last 2 rows 3 (4, 4, 4, 5) times—4 sts.
Work 8 (8, 8, 8, 12)"/20.5 (20.5, 20.5, 20.5, 30.5)cm
I-cord, bind off.

Eye front and back (make 2 with B and 2 with A)

With B and smallest needles, cast on 12 sts.
Row 1 (WS) K1, p10, k1.
Row 2 (RS) Kfb, k10, kfb—14 sts.
Rows 3–6 Rep rows 1 and 2—18 sts.
Rows 7–11, 13, 15 and 17 Work even in St st.
Rows 12, 14, 16 and 18 K1, ssk, k12, k2tog,
k1—dec 2 sts. Bind off.

FINISHING

With RS tog, beg at front edge, backstitch eye
front and back tog, leaving a small opening at the
bottom. Turn RS out and stuff firmly to create a ball
shape. Sew the bottom seam, letting the edges
gather slightly. Sew buttons onto center of eyes. Sew
eyes to top of hat.
Make (2) 6-string tassles and sew to ends of
I-cords. ■

Kitty Hat

Yarn 4
Premier® Yarns Deborah Norville Collection™
Alpaca Dance™, 3½oz/100g balls,
each approx 371yd/340m (acrylic/alpaca)
• 1 (1, 1, 1, 2) balls in Silver Fog #25-16 (A)
• 1 ball in Petal Pink #25-05 (B)

Needles
• One size 7 (4.5mm) circular needle,
16"/40.5cm long *or size to obtain gauge*
• One set (4) size 7 (4.5mm)
double-pointed needles (dpns)

Notions
• Stitch markers
• Tapestry needle
• Small amount of white fingering yarn
• 2 Rhinestone shank buttons

SIZES
Newborn (6–12 mos, 1–2 yrs, 3–5 yrs, 6–10 yrs)

FINISHED MEASUREMENTS
Circumference 12¼ (15¼, 16¾, 18¼, 19)"/31
(38.5, 42.5, 46.5, 48.5)cm

GAUGE
21 sts and 28 rnds = 4"/10cm in St stitch using size
7 (4.5mm) needles.
Take time to check your gauge.

NOTES
1 Choose hat size with circumference 1–2"/2.5–
5cm smaller than actual head circumference.
2 Change to dpns when circumference gets too
small for circulars. The ears, tail, and nose are
worked separately and sew in place.

STITCH GLOSSARY
K2, p2 rib (multiple of 4 sts)
Rnd 1 [K2, p2] around.
Rnd 2 Knit the knits and purl the purls.
Rep rnd 2 for pattern.
Kfbf Knit into front and back of stitch then into
front again—2 st inc.

HAT
With A, cast on 64 (80, 88, 96, 100) sts. Join, being
careful not to twist sts, and pm for beg of rnd.
Work in k2, p2 rib for 8 rnds.
Knit 1 rnd for turning edge.
Work in k2, p2 rib for 8 rnds.
Work even in St st until hat measures 3½ (4¾, 5½,
5¾, 6)"/9 (12, 14, 14.5, 15)cm from knit rnd.

Shape crown
Rnd 1 [K6 (6, 6, 6, 8) sts, k2tog] 8 (10, 11, 12, 10)
times—56 (70, 77, 84, 90) sts.
Rnds 2, 4, 6, 8 and 10 Knit.
Rnd 3 [K5 (5, 5, 5, 7) sts, k2tog] 8 (10, 11, 12, 10)
times—48 (60, 66, 72, 80) sts.
Rnd 5 [K4 (4, 4, 4, 6) sts, k2tog] 8 (10, 11, 12, 10)
times—40 (50, 55, 60, 70) sts.
Rnd 7 [K3 (3, 3, 3, 5) sts, k2tog] 8 (10, 11, 12, 10)
times—32 (40, 44, 48, 60) sts.
Rnd 9 [K2 (2, 2, 2, 4) sts, k2tog] 8 (10, 11, 12, 10)
times—24 (30, 33, 36, 50) sts.
Rnd 11 [K1 (1, 1, 1, 3) sts, k2tog] 8 (10, 11, 12, 10)
times—16 (20, 22, 24, 40) sts.
Rnd 12 [K0 (0, 0, 0, 2) sts, k2tog] 8 (10, 11, 12, 10)
times—8 (10, 11, 12, 30) sts.

Size 6–10 yrs ONLY
Rnd 13 [K1, k2tog] 10 times—20 sts.
Rnd 14 [K2tog] 10 times—10 sts.

All sizes
Next Rnd [K2tog, k0 (0, 1, 0, 0)] 4 (5, 5, 6, 5)
times—4 (5, 6, 6, 5) sts.
Cut yarn leaving a long tail, weave through rem sts,
pull closed and secure end.

KITTY NOSE
With B, cast on 1 st.
Row 1 Kfbf—3 sts.
Rows 2 and 4 Purl.
Row 3 Kfb, k1, kfb—5 sts.
Row 5 Kfb, k3, kfb—7 sts. Bind off.

KITTY EARS (MAKE 2)
Back
With A, cast on 14 sts. Work 4 rows in St st.
Next (dec) row (RS) K1, ssk, k to last 3 sts, k2tog,
k1—2 sts dec. Purl 1 row.
Rep last 2 rows 4 times more—4 sts.
Next (dec) row (RS) Ssk, k2tog—2 sts.
Bind off rem 2 sts.

Front
With B, cast on 12 sts. Work 6 rows even in St st.
Next (dec) row (RS) K1, ssk, k to last 3 sts, k2tog,
k1—2 sts dec. Work 3 rows even.
Rep dec row every other row 3 times more—2 sts.
Bind off rem 2 sts.
With RS tog, backstitch front and back tog, leaving the
bottom edge open. Turn RS out, sew the bottom edge,
cinching tog lightly to curve the ear, and sew in place
on top of hat.

KITTY TAIL
Cut 6 strands of yarn 8"/20cm long. Tie together
and, in groups of two, braid to length. Knot the end.

FINISHING
Turn the ribbing at the turning edge and tack in
place. Sew tail at back of hat, above ribbing. Sew
nose to center front of hat and embroidery mouth as
pictured. Using scrap fingering yarn, embroider whiskers in place next to the nose, as pictured. Use a bit
of hairspray to coat the whiskers stick to the fibers of
the hat if desired. Sew buttons in place for eyes. ■

Wise Old Owl

Yarn 4

Premier® Yarns Deborah Norville Collection™ *Everyday® Soft Worsted*, 4oz/113g balls, each approx 203yd/186m (acrylic)
- 1 (1, 1, 1, 2) balls in Cornflower #100-18 (A)
- 1 ball in Orchid #100-20 (B)
- Small amounts of worsted weight yarn in black, white, and orange

Needles
- One size 8 (5mm) circular needle, 16"/40.5cm long *or size to obtain gauge*
- One pair size 9 (5.5mm) needles

Notions
- Stitch markers
- Tapestry needle

SIZES
Newborn (6–12 mos, 1–2 yrs, 3–5 yrs, 6–10 yrs)

FINISHED MEASUREMENTS
Circumference 11 (14¾, 16½, 17¼, 18¾)"/28 (37.5, 42, 44, 47.5)cm

GAUGE
18¼ sts and 24 rows = 4"/10cm in St st with smaller needles.
Take time to check your gauge.

NOTES
1 Choose hat size with circumference 2–2¾"/5–7cm smaller than actual head circumference.
2 Eyes and nose are worked separately and sewn in place.

STITCH GLOSSARY
Garter St Knit 1 rnd, purl 1 rnd.
Sssk (slip, slip, slip, knit) [Slip 1 st knitwise] 3 times, knit 3 sts tog through the back loops—2 st dec.
K3tog Knit 3 sts tog—2 st dec.
I-cord With dpns, cast on designated number of sts or continue working with rem sts. *Knit one row. Without turning the work, slip the sts back to the beginning of the row. Pull the yarn tightly from the end of the row. Rep from the * as desired. Bind off.

HAT
With A and smaller needles, cast on 50 (66, 74, 78, 84) sts. Join, being careful not to twist sts, and pm for beg of rnd.
Work 2 rnds in garter st.
Change to St st and work even until hat measures 4¾ (6¼, 6¾, 7¾, 7¾)"/12 (16, 17, 19.5, 19.5)cm from cast-on edge. Bind-off, fold flat and seam.

Ear flaps
Mark ear flap placement with stitch markers beneath top corners of hat.
Pick up and knit 16 (18, 18, 18, 20) sts at marker.
Row 1 (WS) K2, p12 (14, 14, 14, 16), k2.
Row 2 (RS) Knit.

Size newborn ONLY
Rows 3–10 Rep rows 1–2 four times more.
Row 11 K2, ssk, k8, k2tog, k2—14 sts.
Row 12 K2, p10, k2.
Row 13 K2, ssk, k6, k2tog, k2—12 sts.

Sizes 6–12 mos (1–2 yrs, 3–5 yrs, 6–10 yrs) ONLY
Rows 3–12 Rep rows 1–2 five times more.
Rows 13, 15 and 17 K2, ssk, knit to last 3 sts, k2tog, k2—Dec 2 sts.
Rows 14, 16 and 18 K2, purl to last 2 sts, k2.

Size 6–10 yrs ONLY
Row 19 K2, ssk, k6, k2tog, k2—12 sts.
Row 20 K2, p8, k2.

All sizes
Row 14 (19, 19, 19, 21) (RS) K2, sssk, k6, k3tog, k2—8 sts.
Row 15 (20, 20, 20, 22) K2, p4, k2.
Row 16 (21, 21, 21, 23) K1, sssk, k3tog, k1—4 sts.
Work 12"/30.5cm I-cord, bind off.

Owl eyes (make 2)
With black scrap yarn and larger needles, cast on 2 sts. Knit 4 rows. Turn piece and pick up 2 sts from the left side, turn again and pick up 2 sts from the cast-on edge, turn again and pick up 2 sts from the right side—8 sts. Join, pm for beg of rnd.
Rnd 1 [Kfb] 8 times—16 sts.
Rnd 2 Knit.
Rnd 3 [Kfb, k1] 8 times—24 sts.

Sizes 1–2 yrs (3–5 yrs, 6–10 yrs) ONLY
Rnd 4 Knit.
Rnd 5 [Kfb, k2] 8 times—32 sts.

All sizes
Rnd 4 (4, 6, 6, 6) Change to white scrap yarn, cut black. Knit.
Rnd 5 (5, 7, 7, 7) [Kfb, k3] 6 (6, 8, 8, 8) times—32 (32, 40, 40, 40) sts.
Rnd 6 (6, 8, 8, 8) Knit.
Rnd 7 (7, 9, 9, 9) [Kfb, k 3 (3, 4, 4, 4)] 8 times—40 (40, 48, 48, 48) sts. Bind off.

Owl nose
With orange scrap yarn and larger needles, cast on 1 st.
Row 1 (WS) [Kfb]—2 sts.
Row 2 (RS) [Kfb] 2 times—4 sts.
Row 3 K1, p2, k1.
Row 4 Kfb, knit to last st, kfb—6 sts.
Rows 5–6 Rep rows 3–4—8 sts. Bind off.

FINISHING
Sew eyes to center front hat, 1–2 rows apart. Sew nose at center front, beneath eyes. Make 2 pompoms in B. Sew to top corners of hat. Make 2 pompoms in A. Sew to ends of I-cord. ■

Mushroom Beret

Jack Deutsch

Yarn 5

Bernat® *Alpaca*™ 3½oz/100g balls, each approx 120yd/110m (acrylic/alpaca)
- 1 (1, 1, 1, 2) balls in Cherry #474502 (A)
- 1 ball in Natural #338934 (B)

Needles
- One size 9 (5.5mm) circular needle, 16"/40.5cm long
- One size 10 (6mm) circular needle, 16"/40.5cm long *or size to obtain gauge*
- One set (4) size 10 (6mm) double-pointed needles (dpns)

Notions
- Stitch markers
- 8 Solid white shank buttons 1¼"/3cm in diameter
- Tapestry needle

SIZES
Newborn (6–12 mos, 1–2 yrs, 3–5 yrs, 6–10 yrs)

FINISHED MEASUREMENTS
Circumference 12 (15, 17, 18, 19)"/30.5 (38, 43, 45.5, 48.5)cm

GAUGE
16 sts and 20 rows = 4"/10 cm in St st with larger needles.
Take time to check your gauge.

NOTES
1 Choose hat size with circumference 1½–2"/4–5cm smaller than actual head circumference.
2 Change to dpns when circumference gets too small for circulars when shaping crown.

STITCH GLOSSARY
K2, p2 rib (multiple of 4 sts)
Rnd 1 [K, p2] around.
Rnd 2 Knit the knits and purl the purls.
Rep rnd 2 for pattern.

HAT
With B and smaller needles, cast on 48 (60, 68, 72, 76) sts. Join, being careful not to twist sts, and pm for beg of rnd.
Rnds 1–6 Work in K2, p2 rib.
Rnd 7 Change to A and larger needles, knit.
Rnd 8 [K2, M1] around—72 (90, 102, 108, 114) sts. Work even in St st until hat measures 2¼ (3¼, 3¼, 4, 4¼)"/5.5 (8.5, 8.5, 10, 11)cm from cast-on edge.

Shape crown
Rnd 1 [K12 (15, 17, 18, 19), pm] around.
Rnd 2 [K to 2 sts before marker, k2tog] 6 times—66 (84, 96, 102, 108) sts.

Rnd 3 Knit.
Rnds 4–7 Rep rnds 2–3—54 (72, 84, 90, 96) sts. Rep rnd 2 until 6 sts rem. Cut yarn leaving a long tail, weave through remaining sts, pull closed and secure.

FINISHING
Sew buttons to top of hat for mushroom spots, as desired. ■